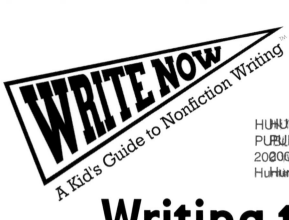

WRITE NOW™
A Kid's Guide to Nonfiction Writing

Writing to
PERSUADE

Jill Jarnow

The Rosen Publishing Group's
PowerKids Press™
New York

Published in 2006 by The Rosen Publishing Group, Inc.
29 East 21st Street, New York, NY 10010

First Edition

Editor: Frances E. Ruffin
Book Design: Emily Muschinske

Photo Credits: Cover and title page © Corbis; p. 5 © Animals in
Action; p. 9 © Photodisc; p. 11 © Corbis; p. 21 © Corbis.

Library of Congress Cataloging-in-Publication Data

Jarnow, Jill.
Writing to persuade / Jill Jarnow.— 1st ed.
     p. cm. — (Write now : a kid's guide to nonfiction writing)
Includes bibliographical references and index.
ISBN 1-4042-2835-7 (lib. bdg.) — ISBN 1-4042-5316-5 (pbk.)
1. English language—Composition and exercises—Study and teaching
(Early childhood) 2. Persuasion (Rhetoric)—Study and teaching (Early
childhood) I. Title. II. Series: Jarnow, Jill. Write now.
LB1139.5.L35J355 2005
372.62'3—dc22
                                              2003018594

Manufactured in the United States of America

Contents

Writing to Persuade

You are a student, but are you also a writer? Your answer should be a strong "Yes!" As a student, much of your time and effort have been and will be spent writing. Being able to write good **nonfiction text** for reports, **essays**, and other kinds of projects can help you to become a better student. Good writers can share their thoughts with others. One style of writing is **persuasive** writing. By writing to **persuade**, you can **encourage** or **convince** people to make an important change. In this book, you will learn the skills to become a **confident** and persuasive writer.

Write a Persuasive Letter

- You and your classmates might decide to send a letter to government leaders to ask them to create a wild animal habitat, or shelter.

- You might write a letter to your school paper to get support to change your school's mascot.

- You could write a note to persuade your parents to let you have a later bedtime.

Dear Mayor Allan,

We are writing to ask if part of North Park could be set aside for a wildlife habitat, or shelter. This habitat would provide food, water, cover, and places for animals to raise their young. The birds and other wild animals that live in and around North Park need to be protected.

Sincerely,

Ms. Wilson's Third Grade Class
The Kennywood School

A Writer's Place

Many people have a favorite place where they can do their best writing. For some, it is at a desk in their room or curled up on their bed. For others, it might be at the kitchen table or at a table in a school or a public library. The idea is to find a place where you feel comfortable and to make it your writing place. Be sure to bring the writing supplies that you will need so that you will not **interrupt** your thoughts in the middle of your work.

Check It Out!

It is a good idea to make a habit of setting aside a certain time of day for doing your homework or for practicing your personal writing.

Your Writing Supplies

In addition to a typewriter or a computer and printer, here are some suggestions for writing supplies that you might like to use:

- ☐ Pencils, pens, and colored markers

- ☐ A pencil sharpener

- ☐ Erasers and correction fluid

- ☐ Paper, a lot of it, including notebooks, writing pads of all sizes, and printer paper, construction paper, and scrap paper

- ☐ Index cards

- ☐ Self-stick notes

- ☐ File folders and a file cabinet, or cardboard, wooden, or plastic boxes for storing your work

What Are the Facts?

When you want to persuade a reader to agree with you, use facts. A fact is a piece of **information** that is known to be true. Facts describe the way something is or the way it used to be. A fact can be proved. For example, it is a fact that the Pacific Ocean is the largest body of water in the world. Another fact is that the cheetah is the world's fastest land animal. By writing to persuade, you can also change a reader's opinion about an issue. An opinion is something people think or feel is true. Some opinions can be based on fact. For example, exercising can be good for your health, and it can be fun to do, too! However, other opinions may not prove to be true.

Fact or Opinion? You Decide.

Here are some facts and some opinions. Can you tell which is which?

1. **Thomas Jefferson was the third American president.** (Fact)

2. **The Moon is the coolest planet.** (Opinion, and not true. The moon is not a planet.)

3. **Komodo dragons are the largest lizards in the world.** (Fact)

4. **Komodo dragons are really scary.** (Opinion based on fact. Komodos can harm people.)

A Persuasive Topic Sentence

How would you let other people know about an idea or a goal? For example, would you like to be a team sports captain? Do you want the class to adopt a pet hamster? Then write a paragraph that persuades people to become interested in your goal or idea. Begin with a **topic** sentence. A topic sentence is usually the first sentence of a **paragraph**. In a persuasive paragraph, the topic sentence may describe your opinions about a subject. The topic sentence also contains the paragraph's main idea. Before you write your topic sentence, make a list of the reasons your idea is a good one.

Writing a Topic Sentence

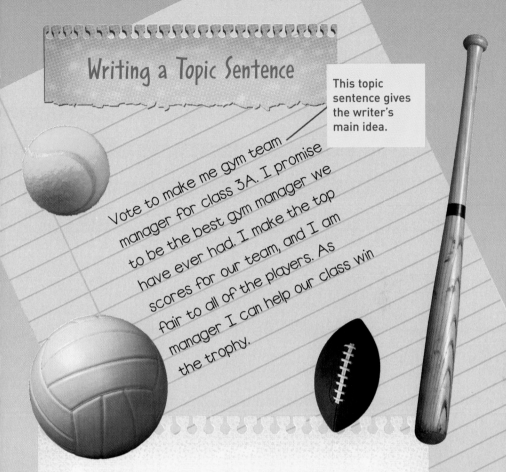

This topic sentence gives the writer's main idea.

Vote to make me gym team manager for class 3A. I promise to be the best gym manager we have ever had. I make the top scores for our team, and I am fair to all of the players. As manager I can help our class win the trophy.

Use one of the subjects below to write a topic sentence that could be used to begin a paragraph that persuades.

1. We want to stay outside and play as late as possible.

2. June is the best month of the year.

3. Soccer can be more fun to play than softball.

Paragraphs That Persuade

All paragraphs, including those that persuade, have three parts. They must have a topic sentence that states the main idea of the paragraph. They must also have several sentences that support the idea and give **details** about the subject. This is called the body. Finally, a paragraph should end with one or more sentences to sum up or close your persuasive argument.

File This...

Your voice is what you use to speak. "Voice" is also a way of "speaking" when you write. It refers to the kinds of words that you choose, and how you use those words in a sentence. Voice also refers to how you use those sentences in a paragraph.

Writing a Paragraph That Persuades

Vote to make Maura O'Brien gym team manager for class 3A.

Topic sentence

She is a good leader and a good athlete who plays many different sports. She is fair with her teammates. She never puts anyone down, and she helps students who are not very good at sports to become better athletes.

Body of the paragraph

If you vote for Maura, she will help to make our class the best team on field day.

Closing sentence

VOTE FOR
Maura O'Brien

A Web That Persuades

Drawing a writing web can help you to **organize** your opinions and ideas. The web on the facing page gives an example of how to organize information you want to include in a persuasive paragraph.

To start, create a box. Choose your topic and write it in the box. Next draw three boxes that connect to the center box. Write three sentences to support your topic in these new boxes. For each support sentence, write three details that back them up. These should be in boxes that connect to the support-sentence boxes. You can use your web to write a well-organized paragraph that persuades.

Why my allowance should be increased.

I send money to charity.

I have more expenses.

I would like to start a savings account.

I want to give to people who need help.

I want to buy gifts for my baby cousin.

I am buying more stamps for my collection.

I give to the library book fund.

I would like more spending money for our family trip.

I have a new pet hamster.

My class is going to adopt a whale.

I am putting aside money for college.

School supplies are more expensive.

Looking at It, Pros and Cons

Have you heard someone say that a subject has its pros and cons? Arguments that are pro are for something. Cons are reasons that are against something. A good way to persuade someone to see your side of an issue is to write a list of pros and cons. Whether you argue for or against something, always back up your discussion with facts. For example, if you would like to persuade your parents to let you stay up later, write a list of reasons you deserve to have a later bedtime. Your parents, however, might reply with a list of reasons that are against your argument.

Weekend Homework Pros and Cons

It is a beautiful Friday afternoon. I have a big school project that is due Monday morning. Should I do the project right away?

Pro: I Should Do It Now

1. I still remember the information we discussed in class today.

2. If I have a problem or a question about the homework, I will have time to find the answers before Monday morning.

3. I will be finished with my homework and I will be free for the rest of the weekend.

Con: I Should Do It Later

1. We spent a long time working on this project in class. I need to take a break from it.

2. This is an important project. I would like to go to the library on Saturday for more information.

3. It is a sunny Friday and I would like to go out and enjoy the afternoon.

Writing a Letter to the Editor

One way to let people know how you feel about an issue is to send a letter to the editor of a local newspaper. Doing this can be an **effective** way of persuading others. Nearly all newspapers, from large, national, and city papers to local and school newspapers, have a Letters to the Editor section. It is a place where people can voice their opinions. Many of these letters have brought about change.

Explain your side of an issue. Describe what you think can be done and how a change can be made. Give examples that can help to prove your point.

Write Now!

Write a letter to the editor of your school newspaper that might persuade someone to make a change in your school.

Letters to the Editor:

Remind the reader of the main idea in the first sentence.

Dear Editor:

Before we move into our new school next August, I would like to suggest changing our mascot. The penguin has been our school mascot for many years. I am suggesting that we make the panther our mascot. Many kids agree with me. Here's why.

Penguins are cute and cuddly animals, and they are great swimmers. However, they don't move well on land, and they can't run very fast. Most of our school's teams play sports that include

running, not swimming. Panthers are very strong, and they're fast. There's another reason. We live in Florida, and penguins are not native to this state. Our state animal is the Florida panther.

As a member of our school's soccer team, I'd like to wear a panther on my uniform.

Thanks,
James Link
Summit Elementary

Give examples that can help prove your point.

State reasons to support your argument.

Using Words That Persuade

Be **enthusiastic**! Using a friendly, positive voice can do a lot to persuade your readers to agree with you. Give readers a hint that you are about to give your opinion by writing, for example, "I think," "I believe," or "I have seen." Use persuasive **verbs**, such as "agree," "help," or "improve." Verbs are words that describe an action or a condition. Choose **adjectives** that are encouraging, such as "best," "exciting," "educational," and "helpful." Avoid writing **phrases** that will make a reader feel foolish. "That's stupid!" and "Everyone knows that!" are examples.

Finding Words That Persuade

Find the words or phrases that persuade in these sentences:

1. I believe that a longer school day will be good for students.

2. We really need to have someone improve our school menu.

3. I urge you to write a letter to the mayor today.

4. I am sure that our team will work harder to win.

ANSWERS:
1. I believe, good
2. We really need, improve
3. I urge
4. I am sure, will work harder

Persuading Others: Four Fun Topics

There is a world of topics with which to practice your persuasive writing skills. Choose one of the following topics. Using facts, write 100 words about the topic to persuade someone to agree with your opinion.

1. Which is the most unusual animal in the world?

2. What is the hardest sport to play?

3. Is the best place for a vacation in the mountains or at the beach?

4. What is the most exciting ride in an amusement park?

   Can you name other fun topics?

Glossary

adjectives (A-jik-tivz) Words that describe a person, a place, or an event.

confident (KON-fih-dent) Having a belief in oneself and one's abilities.

convince (kun-VINTS) To make people believe something.

details (DEE-taylz) Extra facts.

effective (ih-FEK-tiv) Working.

encourage (in-KUR-ij) To give someone reason to do something.

enthusiastic (in-thoo-zee-AS-tik) Happy to do something.

essays (EH-sayz) Short pieces of writing written from a personal point of view.

information (in-fer-MAY-shun) Knowledge or facts.

interrupt (in-tuh-RUPT) To stop in the middle of doing something.

nonfiction (non-FIK-shun) Writing that is about real life.

organize (OR-guh-nyz) To have things neat and in order.

paragraph (PAR-uh-graf) A group of sentences about a certain subject or idea.

persuade (per-SWAYD) To make someone agree to or believe in something.

persuasive (per-SWAY-siv) Able to make someone agree.

phrases (FRAYZ-ez) Groups of words that have a meaning but are missing a subject or a verb.

text (TEKST) The words in a piece of writing.

topic (TAH-pik) The subject of a piece of writing.

verbs (VERBZ) Words that describe actions.

Index

Web Sites

Due to the changing nature of Internet links, PowerKids Press has developed an online list of Web sites related to the subject of this book. This site is updated regularly. Please use this link to access the list:
www.powerkidslinks.com/wnkw/writper/